The Worshipful Companies
Images and Poems from the Norfolk Coast

Stuart Medland

Brambleby Books

The Worshipful Companies
Images and Poems from the Norfolk Coast

Illustration and text copyright © Stuart Medland 2018

All Rights Reserved

No part of this book may be reproduced in any form by photocopying or by any electronic or mechanical means, including information, storage or retrieval systems, without permission in writing from both the copyright owner and the publisher of this book.

Stuart Medland has asserted his right under the Copyright, Design and Patent Act, 1988, to be identified as author of this work.

A CIP catalogue record for this book is available from the British Library.

ISBN 9781908241603

My thanks to Pensthorpe Natural Park and in particular to Chrissie Kelley for the opportunity to photograph the front cover Ruff at such close quarters.

Published 2018 by
Brambleby Books Ltd., UK
www.bramblebybooks.co.uk

Cover design and layout by Tanya Warren, Creatix Design

Printed and bound by FINIDR, Czech Rep.

FSC and PFSC accredited

The Worshipful Companies
saltmarsh, grazing meadow, creek, pool, scrape & dune

To my Grandchildren
and to Isabella who is ten

Prelude

The Worshipful Companies continues in the vein of the first of this series of Norfolk Wildlife Encounters – *Rings in the Shingle* – insofar as it is composed of a personal and somewhat random choice of subjects dictated by the photographs I have taken during my wanderings and the inspiration they have been to me to write. It is by no means definitive, though I do hope representative of the wildlife of the particular habitats met within the scope of this book. I trust the reader will not be too disappointed in failing to find a species he or she might have expected to – though it may well be worth looking within the pages of the previous volume – there being, necessarily, a happy overlap between the two, resulting in several arbitrary distinctions which the birds themselves will not have been aware of!

The poetry here has often sprung directly from the photograph itself or the photo may have rather served to draw me back into an encounter in order to investigate it further and reflect upon it. Either way, the photo is integral to the poem and not simply an illustration of it. The accompanying prose assumes a slightly more important role, it seems, within this second book – a third point to the triangle which serves perhaps more readily to balance up the other two.

About the Author

Stuart Medland has been writing poetry inspired by the natural world from boyhood. Since retiring from teaching he has been able to devote himself more fully to a literary and photographic exploration of the North Norfolk that he has come to know and love so well – which has culminated in this *Encounters with Norfolk Wildlife* series of celebrations of its many and diverse habitats. *The Worshipful Companies* is the second in that series, following on from the inaugural *Rings in the Shingle*.

Stuart is also author of three un-illustrated volumes of poetry; *Last Man Standing*, a collection in memory of his father, *Nonesuch*, in celebration of his friendship with naturalist David Stapleford, and *Ouzel on the Honister*, inspired by his long-time association with the Lake District where he now lives with his partner, Beth.

Stuart's creative impulse finds further scope for expression in his bird paintings which explore the shapes and patterns made by the various flocks of waders and wildfowl encountered in his books and which may usually be seen at the Birdscapes Gallery in Glandford, near Holt in North Norfolk.

Contents

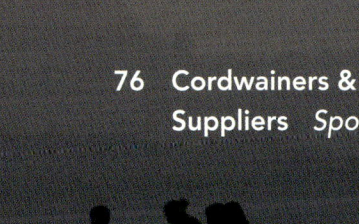

9 **Foreword**

11 **The Worshipful Companies**
(Title Poem)

12 **Scriveners & Notaries**
Lapwings

16 **Wax Chandlers**   *Avocets*

22 **Gold Wyre Drawers**
Golden Plovers

26 **Paviors (highway repairers), Watermen & Lightermen**
Brent Geese

30 **Fletchers & Bowyers**   *Curlews*

36 **Peepers & Whistleblowers**

44 **Mercers & Haberdashers**
Dunlin

48 **Fishers & Crabbers**
Egrets

52 **Apothecaries, Grinders of Powders & Suppliers to Sawbones**
Shoveler, Teal & Pintail

58 **Bon Coiffure & Haute-Couture Artistes**   *Ruff*

62 **Girdlers & Spinners**
Pink-footed Geese

66 **Keeners & Sharpeners & Maritime Adventurers**
Common & Arctic Terns

70 **Town Cryers**
Redshanks

76 **Cordwainers & Shoehorn Suppliers**   *Spoonbills*

80 **Quilters & Broderers**
Greenshanks

82 **Loriners (manufacturers of bridle, bit & spur)** *Snipe*

88 **Barstaff & Bottlewashers**
Shelduck

90 **Leapers & Moongazers**
Brown Hares

96 **Dune Bathers & Floaters**
Grayling, Wall, Painted Ladies & Dark-green Fritillaries

104 **Furriers & Small Mammal Re-packagers**
Short-eared Owls

The Worshipful Companies

Striding-out Avocet

Foreword

The interlinking theme of this, the second in the series of photo-poetic *Norfolk Wildlife Encounters*, is that of the Medieval Guilds or Companies – each with its own colourful, often flamboyant, livery and proud esoteric tradition – which to my mind have such a striking and quite thrilling correlation with the plumage, the group identity and social organisation of our teeming winter flocks of waders and wildfowl. Moreover, it is often when this large number of diverse and various species from different parts of the globe are co-mingling within their shared habitats, each to its niche and seemingly oblivious to one another, that I am most impressed by this utterly partisan sense of community.

Within this overall scheme I have included one or two species which have somewhat looser affiliations with their own kind, but it has still been a happily imaginative exercise to draw similar parallels with what were essentially the original crafts and trades unions.

There are butterflies here as well among the dunes, which there simply wasn't room for within the pages of *Rings in the Shingle* – and hares, familiar and always emotive creatures which yet have mystical associations and connections with the land predating by far the Medieval Guilds.

Sales of *The Worshipful Companies* will continue to support the work of the CATS Foundation in raising awareness of and funding research into potential treatments for the progressive neurological disorder known as Tay-Sachs. To find out more or to help in any way, please contact www.cats-foundation.org.

The Worshipful Companies

Each guild his own; though every bird
no more his own man than the next.

Ancient-and-modern; craft and mercantile,
grubbing profession – every piping call or
cheering and horizon-darkening chorus, every
bubbling-up of marshy song, a music-making

Livery to match their pride-swell,
customary and tradition-steeped –
their differentiating – cut and colour.

Every company a closed-shop, open;

Noisesome, multitudinous and ever
nose-to-nose and shoulder-rubbing,
trample-toe Societies of Secrets – every
guild as blind and deaf to every other one
as if their trade or craft was all
the air, the water and the mud had
need of and all vaguely tolerated
(suchlike similar-familiars
but fillers-of-a-space). So

Scriveners and bowyers (longbow makers)
watermen and lightermen, apothecaries,
master mariners and merchant tailors (who
swap pecking order with the merchant
skinners once a year), wax chandlers, vintners,
pewterers, cordwainers, curriers (tanned leather
dressers), coopers, fletchers, drapers, farriers and
basketmakers, girdlers, armourers and brasiers,
and founders (bronze and brass) then pattenmakers
(wooden shoe) and loriners (the bit, the bridle and the spur)
with haberdashers, goldsmiths – or their

Very bird equivalents – engaged upon their
Mystery plays in one
continuous performance
and throughout the Season on

The saltmarsh and the creek, the
grazing meadow and its own meander
into pool and scrape, the Sea's bank; every

Corporation's blue-sky, raining-sky
and snow-filled, livery hall.

Scriveners and Notaries

The name 'Lapwing' is a happy corruption of the Anglo-Saxon *hleapewince* which means, literally, 'run-and-wink' and perfectly describes their stop-and-start perambulations whilst also conveying a sense of their flip-flop flight. They have the distinction of possibly the greatest number of local and traditional names ascribed to them of any of our birds – including Peewit, Green Plover and my own favourite, Hornpie, which conjures up wonderfully, I think, the light and dark contrast of their plumage as well as the quill-like crest.

Lapwings are one of our truly resident plovers and are traditionally associated with the arable countryside – where they are apparent in wintertime, distributed evenly throughout the furrowed fields and all facing the same way into wind, rain or snow – as well as on our coastal and wetland marshes. Their daredevil, tumbling display flight, accompanied by what I always imagine to be squeaky bath-toy noises, is one of the joys of early Spring. The clown-like facial markings of Lapwings, their bouncing wisp of a crest on a box-kite head, their big paddle wings as well as the iridescent sheen upon their shoulders, which throws back purple, turquoise and even magenta from a shimmering green, combine to make these birds utterly distinctive and one of our island treasures.

The Mudpool Scrivener image is my favourite photo of an individual Lapwing, the good light enchantingly capturing all its salient features as well as the mascara on its eyelashes – soap in the eyes – while it glances over its shoulder as if to anticipate some question I might have about its preference for such a mud-pool environment.

Mudpool Scrivener

Larger feet have trampled here; hoof-pools in the pool-already with an onerous and heavy-handed sentencing.

And so the scrivener, who would be only ever
small-time magisterial upon this muddy bench
and lenient in his own empty-courtroom pantomime,
with powdered wig and liner for the public eyes
and in the judges silks left hanging on the door;
chrysanthemum and greengage, sage
and damson satin brushstrokes – oil
upon the water – and important in his
own right at the day's end in among
his crowding, eager reedy-quills.

With inky-whiskered flourish
he will write off each and every
minor misdemeanour of the marsh.

No more the minion copyist with
pufferfish and box-kite head
bent over with his keeping-up
too often cuffed all up the back of it
with chiding from the judge
up on his feet again; soap

In the eyes, wet behind the ears
and squeezy yet with all his
bath-toy-squeaky cries.

And squeakier yet
with nib upon the page.

Lapwing Draggle

The wind is unbending, bending the birds.

Here they come – draggle and straggle, all flop-flip and flip-flop and tumble-dice-out-of-a-beaker, with everyone's chromosomes troubling to double (like jumpers pulled inside-out over the head) and now

Windmilling, lolly-pop signalling (old Morris Minor) each bird another, undoing, unscrewing this instant and dropping through holes in the sky to the grass-streaming deck and squeezed by this low pressure rain-pumping cloud into 'all of us overboard!' cries.

Oddfellow flying. Their Worshipful Company liveries, piebald and orange and green; the Order of Lapwings, of Peewits, of Hornpies, of Plovers in Green.

On the Scrape

Operatic stand-ins
crowding-up the bare-board wings – or
extras in a Noel Coward play,

The Lapwings wait about in
gold-edged smoking jackets of
resplendent greens,
slick-haired and with a
cigarette in silver holder –
wing in one pocket.

Some are the bounders of the piece
(their masks already slipping)

Who confront the audience
with sudden villainous intent, or

Face-on, Hector-helmeted
(the hero in disguise)

Or simply diabolical.

Wax Chandlers

This is the bird to get one hooked. With that impossibly fine and re-curved beak, the Paris-catwalk elegance – that simple and essential style – Avocets, for me, are still an endless source of fascination, of visual and of artistic satisfaction.

Their re-establishment as a breeding species at Minsmere in Suffolk in the 1950s and '60s is often credited as being the single most important factor behind the popular resurgence in watching birds and in public interest in, and awareness of, conservation issues. I was caught up in the excitement of all that in my early teens, though I didn't see my first Avocet until some twenty years later by which time the floodgates had opened and Avocets had spread by their own volition throughout both Suffolk and Norfolk and were a real success story. That did nothing to dampen my very first excited gasp of appreciation, and even though they are now a common sight hereabouts during the Spring and Summer, I still look forward eagerly to (though am often caught out by) the return of the birds from their winter quarters not that far away and mainly in the Hayle estuary in Cornwall where it is evidently a degree or two warmer.

An iconic bird if ever there was one, probably by now on a par with the Robin or the Golden Eagle. One to which we readily attach such ephemeral human attributes as charm and grace as well as beauty – though the truth is somewhat more down to earth; they are quite pugnacious birds in fact, irritable even – to ascribe just a couple more human qualities to them! (Aggression amongst themselves is very interestingly ritualised into a group circle or semi-circle display in which each pair confronts another whilst posturing with heads low down and beaks to the ground. Quite a spectacle.)

I am pleased with the main image (page opposite) on several levels. Firstly, there is the story that it seems to tell by way of the body language of the birds; her 'for one night only' invitation, his 'can I be bothered – yet again?' Secondly, the pair's reflections, redolent – especially his, all concertina-floppy – of a Salvador Dali painting. Thirdly, the lack of differentiation between the background and the foreground which tends to throw the birds forward, giving them back their free-standing quality and drawing attention only to that single moment caught between them.

The Avocet standing over her egg and so oblivious to me not half a dozen yards away is the very first bird photo I took which I thought worth keeping (see page 19). The seemingly high-wire intensity of her devotion inspired me to its poem, again the first of such I imagined worthy of retaining and which itself gave rise, later, to the very idea of a collection of poems and photos such as this. The photo, which I took at Pensthorpe Waterfowl Park (as it was then called), is not the sharpest I've ever taken, but its very significance, I do believe, warrants its inclusion. I have a lot to be thankful to this young Avocet for!

Indelicate Company

You may if you wish.

I might. In a minute. Didn't
you ought to be playing a
little bit harder to get?
You know – not so
promiscuous, not in my –
as it were – face?

Is that what you'd like, Dearest?
Should I be more of a tease?
Should I do lingerie?
Feminine mystery?

Now that you mention it.

Haven't we been there, though?
Done that and both got the T-shirt?
All of those tiresome and time-honoured niceties, all-
round-the-houses preliminaries? Don't
you remember? This isn't about
you-and-me anymore. This is
lights, camera, action!'

Eggs? Skinny nestlings?
Commitment!

Something like that. Now,
let's give it one more shot – what do you say?
For the sake of the Programme, the picture that's
bigger, the gene pool, our small contribution
to natural selection – mmm? Shall we?

Or are you not up to it, Dearest?

Thumbprint

Her head is a thumbprint

Rolled from the back of
one of my own –

Over and up, a
rocking-horse,
see-sawing seal –

To press an identity
on her. I lift it again

And again. She

Bobs at me. I am
a darkening smudge
on her water and sky
as she does so. An
arms-and-legs blot.

All my distinguishing
features are easily
lost on her.

Egg & Avocet

(*About the size and weight of a soul*)

Round and round she
rises and she falls
upon her clockwork.

I am smitten.
I am all attention.

So delicately pained to do this properly –
in her un-practice – that I feel I ought to look away
for shame that I am simply voyeur to a
nursing mother in her modesty and at her
broken-legged ballet.

But I can't. At last she
sets her callipers of
eyelash-bent piano wire
to a spark-plug gap –

And finds her endless saltmarsh world has
shrunk to the horizons of an egg; they
tingle with her fine adjustments
(like the buzz of paper
through a comb upon your lips).

She cannot
for one moment
let this be.

Today, we will not see
how well her blind-man-hopeful stick
may sweep the water carefully to ribbons,
how the whole sky
lingers after her.

*The ink that runs
has learned to walk
and now she dares italics
all along her hairline-fracture nib,
roundly prints her
woodcut black and white
upon me. So it is.*

She hovers, tantalising, like a
shingle heat-haze – on the very limit of possession –
raising all the downy hairs upon my skin,

Unwittingly, the perfect
airy-trembling fit between
my eggshell palms,

The attic-dry
and salt-sweet
toast of feathers
to my nose –

About the size
and weight
of a soul.

The Worshipful Companies

That very first photograph (see page 16)

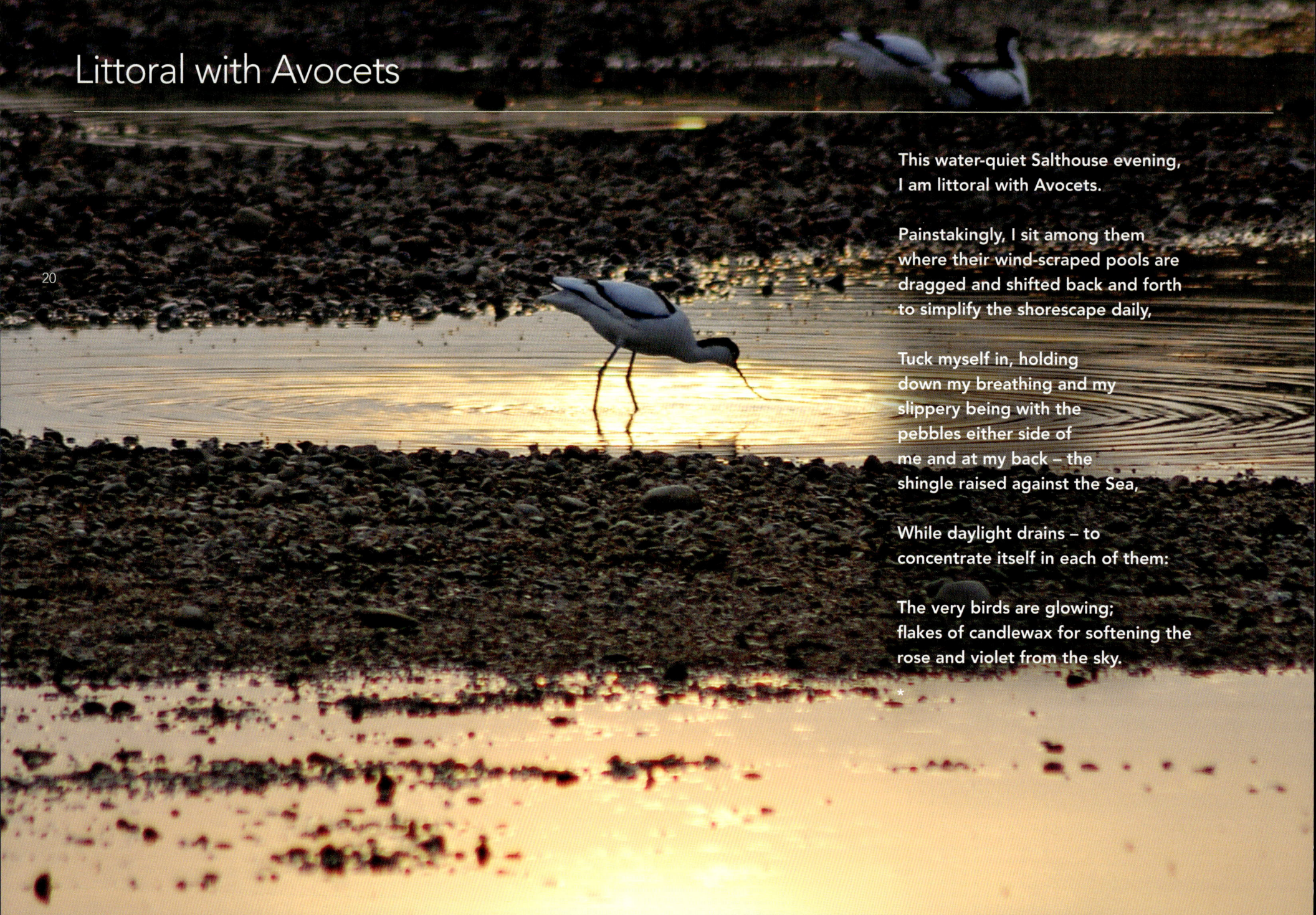

Littoral with Avocets

This water-quiet Salthouse evening,
I am littoral with Avocets.

Painstakingly, I sit among them
where their wind-scraped pools are
dragged and shifted back and forth
to simplify the shorescape daily,

Tuck myself in, holding
down my breathing and my
slippery being with the
pebbles either side of
me and at my back – the
shingle raised against the Sea,

While daylight drains – to
concentrate itself in each of them:

The very birds are glowing;
flakes of candlewax for softening the
rose and violet from the sky.

*

The Worshipful Companies

One by one they genuflect their
long blue legs away –
folding down their walking,
quaintly cantilever,
unspilled jug – and then think
better of it and go
tilting at the windmill on the
Don Quixote shiny water,

Lilting blithely through it,
skinning it, alive of midges, with an
oscillating sweep of
upturned-eyelash beak 'til

All at once they're
downing tools to hoe-and-
shovel-off a gull intruder with a
sudden 'kleeping' chorus,
like a snowplough, altogether.

*

Somehow, I am not intruding – every
nodding head in their
balletic bobbing is a
fingerprint of thumb
jerked back into my eye
to keep me wakeful of them.

One high-stepping bird reminds me of a
clown-on-stilts who's handing out the
invitations to this evening's circus,
kneeling with his elbows for us.
I have had mine early, clearly.

Or they fly on tiptoe,
stretching out their white-from-black to
wind a blurry ribbon-circle round me.

*

Lapwings clown the sky themselves.

The Sandwich Terns are sharpening the sea wall
all the way up to the Point and
cranking up the evening one more notch.

Turnstones fidget with their own reflections,
nonplussed, not un-naturally, this end of the day.

A harrier drifts high enough to mediate a flight path
through these noising birds which seem to feel the need to flock,

And now a spare dog blurts an oystercatcher from
its patch of Sea Convolvulus,

Whilst I am littoral
with Avocets.

Cley windmill is the one referred to.

Gold Wyre Drawers

The gold-mantled, ermine-bordered black of a male Golden Plover in full breeding regalia is a (pretty much Scottish Highlands') sight to behold – and similarly the Grey Plover whose name does not at all do justice to the silver effect of its own embroidered coat. (I wonder why it's not known more widely as the Silver Plover?) In Norfolk we see these birds only at the turn of their seasons, in eclipse plumage as it's known, before they don their winter-mourning feathers, which are a very watered-down version and the black and precious-metal contrast is lost. What we do see of the Golden Plovers, however, is arguably every bit as impressive, for their en-masse aerial displays above our winter pools and grazing meadows – with plenty of differentiation still between their new pale tummies and their washed-out gold – are amongst the most stunning and spectacular in the northern hemisphere.

Like many before me, I have been fascinated, captivated, not to say besotted by that switch from light to dark and back again as they twist and turn in orchestrated spasm, filter back through one another to seeming-stall and flicker in apparent indecision and then begin again. Attempting to capture these moments of changeover, when one half of the flock is but the peak and the trough of a light wave behind the other is one photographer's challenge which I never grow tired of.

It's probably true to say that I enjoy taking this kind of photograph most of all. All one can do when a whole flock of birds such as this decides to take off is to try to remain focused on one small part and stay with them, though this is actually the essence of wildlife photography for me; that intimate involvement in the vital and dynamic endeavour of every individual bird – whose story becomes apparent only when looking back through frame after frame later on – through the act of attempting to capture the whole brief event. It feels like a privilege, a welcome onboard – an encounter which unreservedly includes.

The Whole Sky Sprinkles

The whole sky sprinkles –

Mother-of-pearl and
gold-leaf in tatters –
sparkles with grains
of sand through
bright rain, sprung

Handclaps of
needlepoint, flip
revolutions of
dark-flashing-light; the
seeds of the daytime
sown deep in the night.
(Oh, those dark
Northern Lights).

Flung open – a
gloved fist of
sandstorm and seaspray,
now snatched to a close
to blind and to mystify –

(All this in-front of me,
quick-contradictory,
turn-turtle alchemy.)

Such is this hemisphere
shrunk to my pupil;
a gimlet for birdlife
in-thrall to its gravity –
out of its black hole
blown, starry all over
New Heavens of sky.

The Sky Filled with the Field

The sky is empty
   and I did not see it empty;

Vacant as the marsh below a minute since,
    which I saw drawn of all its gold-point thousands
       by the harrier's lodestone eye –
    a silent, iron-filing rush, all

Lifted like a rope still dripping with each single bird
   out of a wet-green sea, now thrumming
      to a steel-wire tightness
         with a shock of finer rain.

             *

All afternoon,
    along the hay-weave emerald, along
       thin bolts of blue, they've
          fidgeted to edge a tapestry
              in pearl and antique gold, have

Quilted-up the soggy ground –
   a feather-blown and shifting carapace of bird;
     small tortoise groups to push along the line of
       tiny Roman knocking shoulders, spilling treasures.
         White-enamelled goblets rolled upon their sides.

             *

Then, as I watched, the
   sky filled with the field with
      one long pull of the harrier's oar – its
         swing away-and-clear, its turn and plunge again, which

Stirred them through the sky so wholly
    that I even thought I heard the crack of canvas as the
        onshore wind ballooned them –
            loose and blowy-rigging –
                caught them hard and lifted them away.

Light spangled dark, unwitting
    with the whole flock set-fair sunward to
        collapse, for need of boggy marsh again –
            dark, spangled light

Until the first half of them passed back through the second
    on some wanton impulse which sent panic
        coursing through the blizzard-whirling flock – night

Terrors by the light of day, in every bird's mind's eye; of snowy owls,
    of fledglings running in small circles with no hiding place
        beneath a shrinking, dead-weight shadow.

            *

And now that is empty, too.

But for the harrier. I look up.

It is me and me alone that sits inside his shadow and
    my capstan head that he is winding coils of quayside rope around to
        pull himself hard in – and my skull that he's
            banging on the inside of, round all four corners,

'Til I spot the stoat – the
    patchy-ermined, thumb-eared bolt of
        chilly-blooded mammal such-as-I, now standing,
            hands as innocent as if in pockets, now
                at the sight of me, fur-slippery
                    down the dyke-side bank.

The harrier shrugs big wings
    and floats away to stretch his fingers and for all I know
        to 'crack his knuckles' as he does.

I've served no useful purpose here at all, it seems.

            *

I lean back in amongst the hills of moles
    and puzzle at a slight discolouration, at the
        faintest stain – no more – upon the underbelly of the sky;
            a tingling spraint of shadow
                which is lightening or intensifying
                    with my very breathing.

It is all the plovers – rarefied,
    as whisper as the breath of gnats.

My mind has goose-bumps
    with imagining what they must see from such a height;
        a tangled thread of tide-line water on a cotton spool
            from Cromer all the way around the corner to the Wash,
                the shinglebank, a welt – the length of skipping rope –
                    at pains to hold the Sea until it heals, the
                      pasture-marsh, an elongated silver coin of rain,
                        like homely tundra pools that blink their own
                          worth ever back at them.

Paviors (highway repairers), Watermen & Lightermen

It was the Brent Geese which most astonished me chasing my first winter in Norfolk. I wondered afterwards how any winter sky could be complete without them; their dark, unbridled skeins seemed always on the move from one part of the saltmarsh to another – the white of their undertails aflare – from one arable field or pasture to a similar but miles away and to the unenlightened mind no more or less attractive. Paviors – repairers of the highways of the sky that are their own. Tarmacadam-plumaged, bumpy rumble-strip upon the grass, a thousand milling birds – their multifarious and subtle shades of browning-grey from silvery graphite through to anthracite and blackest bitumen.

My heart lifts at that first intimation of a puzzling breakaway horizon over the mudflats sometime in September and for a moment I cannot place that undertone of intermittent throaty yaps and yap responses – like a too familiar, overlapping liturgy – and here they come and are over my head again, their white neck bands apparent, dark eyes shining in a darker head, with an ear-licking creaking of wings.

We are fortunate to have them. These little geese which breed in the Arctic tundra but can hardly wait to get back to us, it seems, nearly died out in the 1930s due to a sudden lack of Eel Grass, their winter staple, so that they have had to learn to supplement their diet with young cereal crops (which does little to endear them to landowner farmers, of course), while the Eel Grass still recovers.

I like the idea of the Brent Geese being also akin to the old watermen and lightermen; firstly in their great fondness for sitting on the water and cluttering-up the creeks just when the seal boats are ready to go out and then for the essential and unfussy light and darkness of them – dusk-plumaged with their white sterns lit, though only at a stretch.

I like the main photograph for its horizontal depth – the sense that the geese are stretched across the sky in their familiar plane and that, indeed, I might be flying with them, rather than the whole flock passing by.

The image of the four geese flying – three young birds and a single adult – I am pleased with for its illustration of their many shades of grey made happily apparent by the daylight glancing off them at exactly the right angle for my camera to pick up. So often with dark bird subjects it is difficult to record such subtle differentiations. I have often imagined making a pencil drawing from this photo with all the various depths, the hardnesses and softnesses, of graphite, lined up at my elbow – along with an eraser!

27

On the Saltmarsh

Light crowds.

Dark crowds back
   and bullish.

Skins of pool-water
    side-saddle after one another – mouth-froth
      spume on my cheek.

Wind is cut glass – flint-knife edged – and
    scarifying grasses to a thread, whittling the
      once shrubby Seablite
        down to the bone.

My own cornea shines and weeps and
   squeezes hard to see again.

        *

The sky is also purple – and the Watch House
   on its miles-long slappy plank of stage
     is bouncing on it like a plywood prop
       spontaneously applauded by a
        glare of big white sun –
         substantial, for a
          single moment while

The shifting shingle seawall
   gags a roar (a dried-pea
      snake to stop a hurricane).

        *

A sound above a sound above a sound.

The air is thickening.
     Is gathering a noise.

And now the sky unbuttons – thousands at a time – with Arctic Geese.
    Black Brent Geese,
        pupil-flickering uncountable and
          quickly silting up the winter air with

Hearty bickering; a
    strident, doggy cheer, an
       overflowing-drainpipe babble –
        excitation, at their
         spent migration.

Now misfiring, running out of steam,
    the teeming birds begin to drop – a
       word below a word below a word upon a page –

To button up again
   so we are hard of hearing,
     tired of reading,

Simmering the pasture grass with
    murmurations of embarrassment at
      having made a din, at having
        no-one to receive them but themselves –

At having come to crowd out
    yet another winter's meagre light
      which it can ill afford.

Too Long Here

(*The Brent Geese*)

The Worshipful Companies

A cinder cloud – crushed

Drawing charcoal
splintered onto wetted
watercolour paper, races,
breath-cold, all around
the surface of my eye.

Now March and still not gone.
The Brent Geese, too long on the saltmarsh,
stuck together like a Winter Mixture
too long in the jar, conglomerated, only black
as part-sucked Liquorice Imps

And wearing, sad, their thread-pulled-and-
unravelling old cardigans, their saggy-nappy
pants – their socks-for-necks now slipping,
concertina-round-the-ankles,
from their ring-pull bangles,

Heads still up the dark-cloud flue.

They stand, as suddenly alert and twisty-headed
as a courtroom barrister, and to a man

All rise – although there is no Justice to be seen
but for this empty-headed wig of crumpled snow – and

Only slip-masked highwaymen –
a dozen Lapwings – in the gallery behind.

Regardless, every day, their
case for staying, heard.

Fletchers & Bowyers

I have only recently come to a realisation that the cry of the Curlew is a sound I could never possibly grow weary of hearing; so wobblingly musical is it, so all-at-once intriguing, so ventriloquist and so attuned to the pitch of human yearning and the unapologetic need for answers. It is an existential voice. It is the one essential ingredient (sincere apologies to Redshanks, Brent Geese, Shrubby Seablite, mud and water) of the working winter saltmarsh.

Curlews are enigmas; I find them contradictory in themselves. They embody, seemingly, in the way they fill their own space absolutely, the very ideal of a solitary, self-contained, quite-happy-with-one's-own-company, thank you very much, existence and yet one might quite easily come across a whole flock of twenty or so, in serious convocation, just around the corner; a hermit conference. So assuredly large and so full of gravitas does their character appear that smaller waders and shorebirds seem to be magnetically attracted to them. I have quite often seen a single Redshank, or Ringed or Grey Plover, Turnstone, the odd Oystercatcher even, apparently hypnotised by their eremite presence and simply transfixed or quite unable not to tag along. The original working title for this book was in actual fact 'The Worshipful Company of Curlews' specifically, before it occurred to me that the idea of such an arcane guild or secret society co-operative might well apply to all the other saltmarsh species in their flocks.

Talking of which – Fletchers, for the dart-flight patterning let loose upon their underbelly, just before it turns to white (such variations on a theme within their first-glance chaff-strewn plumage, such leathery slaps of dark and light from those big wings); – Bowyers, yes, for that iconic, lugworm-slurping, rollercoaster beak!

We have related birds, known as Whimbrels, also on the Norfolk coast in winter. These are superficially like Curlews but a great deal rarer; you have to go further north than the Lakes or Pennines to come across Whimbrels breeding, though Orkney is a good place and where I've come across them two-a-penny in the treeless fields. They are slightly smaller wading birds, their beaks less curved with not so far to go. A black-striped crown is their distinctive feature. Both birds have a white rump which is strikingly visible in flight and something of a surprise when seen for the first time.

I have dedicated the poem 'Old Morston Curlews' to Ted Hughes who is my foremost inspiration as a wildlife poet. His own description of Curlews as 'twists of near-inedible sinew' ('Curlews Lift' from *Remains of Elmet*) gave my imagination free and suddenly legitimate rein as a young man and it still informs my every walk upon the moor and marsh.

I like the 'Pop Curlew' photograph because of the dynamic visual absurdity of the bird's long-evolved camouflage up against the primary red, white and blue. It's interesting to speculate on how aware such a bird (or animal) might be of its own conspicuity when in an alien (in this case, busy habour-staithe) environment through its own choice. The image somehow has the quality of a holiday or railway poster illustrative of the happy co-existence of Man at work & play and bird-stroke-beast along the Norfolk coast and for this reason came quite close to being the cover of the book.

The 'Curlew Ablutions' I enjoy for its quirkiness, which brings out another side of the bird's character, and for the fact that its toilet theme is redolent of the somewhat dishevelled state in which the Curlews return to the marsh after raising their families up on the moors – often with missing flight and tail feathers and in thorough need of a good wash and brush-up as well as a moult!

The main image for 'Gilded Curlews' I like especially for the evening's gold leaf rubbed with infinite care upon each of the feathers of the bird and wrinkled on the surface of the very mud itself. Light is everything – as they say!

The Worshipful Companies

Gilded Curlew

How the purpose, striding,
creek-light bouncing from the eye.

How the gown, mud-fabricated,
gold and silver threaded
with the last-glance sun, how

Navigating at the end of callipers to
measure and to mark upon a
mind-map of his own, the gentle,
saucer-shallow, soft-suck,

World-without-an-end horizons.

How the purpose, striding.

Pop Curlew

Out on the marsh, this
Curlew keeps me at a
long-arm's distance
(out of place but still
parading his identity)
upon the short legs of
his own unwritten law;
a channel creek apart
and he and I apace and
throwing backward
glances. Classic

Curlew. On his own
terms, though, and
at a saunter up the
draining staithe, I am
a different proposition;
one more set of
indeterminable and
yet harmless colours in
their odd confinements
on the harbour water.
Last Night of the Proms.
Red, white and blue.
As near to pop as
this here bird will do.

Down in the Wells Creek,
not a stone's throw
from the fish & chips,
another Curlew mopes and
mithers in among the
dinghy mooring ropes laid
loose across the sizzling mud
with lowly spirit tread. This
one as close to hangdog
as a bird can be with having
prostituted all his other-
worldliness for table scraps.

Crossed-over Curlew.
Touchable Untouchable.
Too far gone and
no way back by now.

Old Morston Curlews (*for Ted Hughes*)

Curlews, lately re-conditioned –

Bent back into shape, beaks
wrapped around a gritstone anvil –

Down from the Pennine bleak.

Rise, all irate and bellicose, swing their
big-freckled, Wesleyan forearms

Out across the saltmarsh; High Peak

Smithies ringing in their ears, the
cry and answering moorland bleat (all
tremulous within a world of water now).

I sense their landlord grudge and dudgeon at these
summer-indolent, unprofitable tenancies.
Their holiday lets, let go. At once

They are all rolled-up trouser legs and
shirt sleeves, dragging billhook grooves
through sizzling creeks to clear the season's
green-slime clog, the silt and choke – the

Crazy-paving mud now turning over either side
to black and shining polythene – and all the while

Admonishing, with ever-quickening
finger-wagging from some hidden purslane-pulpit,
wastrel talents buried in the ooze, not used, the sins of
pleasure-seeking by the half-mile queue, the

Devil's sloth in keeping not a worthy seep of tide.

Tatterdemalion (Diary, July 30th)

The year has turned. Already. August is the tail between the legs of

Summer. All is done, exhausted. Parenting is red to the knuckle, last gasp and worn to the bone.

Tatterdemalion, the Curlews are straggling back from the Moor.

Aplonk – to astonish the marsh – in the purslane and lavender, hardly a flight feather left to their name, the offspring they've dragged from the top of the World all

Bewildered and gangling as overgrown pheasant chicks, quickly secreted in side-creeks and out of the way for the morning. Limivorous. Only

Admonished in general with 'What did I say to you?' finger-wag burbles which start with a chiding and end with the bubble-glug song of the wilderness.

Corked curlews.
Curlews un-corked.

The Worshipful Companies

Mud to Mud

Limivorous, with tip-top mechanism – mud to mud and back again upon a curlew-mindset trigger spring.

Faceful and drag, faceful and drag it again; no

Sanderling, Redshank or Dunlin-like dashes to

Dashes – but evermore, head in the hands and

Mud unto mud.

Odd Curlew God

Diary, October 28th

This morning, oddly, curlews fly around my head at half a saltmarsh sweep but clearly bent upon returning.

I begin to wonder if the tidewrack-purslane shade of jacket I am wearing and the telephoto lens which dangles from my neck much like a lengthy beak, as well as my more measured plod, with time to spend this morning, has imagined them a curlew deity set foot upon the saltmarsh to invite their full-blown worship or a simple nod of deference – whichever

Is their preference.

Peepers & Whistleblowers

The presence of the winter Wigeon here is inescapable. From the moment of arrival on the grazing meadows and the marsh they are the underlying background theme to all its music – to its very quality and tone; a naïve and minimalist ping-pong whistling which always sounds to me like telling tales and after a long day out can seem to border on inanity! Wigeon are apron-string ducks which graze like geese and altogether at a pace as if they'll be called in from play at any minute, taking off, en masse, as if anticipating being reprimanded and returning to the same spot, all a-buzz.

For all that, the palette of the males' plumage, together with the edgings of the feathers of the wings at rest, is quite delightful – from that stub-little, silver-grey beak with its peep, through the liver-pink chest to the black and white stern. The pale gold slick of feathers swept back over the rusting-chestnut head is utterly convincing aesthetically, I think, and quite distinctive.

Fair game to wildfowlers, the numbers of our Wigeon are now such that they are able to sustain such 'thinnings-out' of the population in the name of sport.

With the mirror image of a clear blue winter sky imparting the quality of runny paint to the pool water, the reed reflections gilding it, this small flotilla of wildfowl is shown off to gorgeous effect, the delicately mottled brown females providing the perfect buffer for the males between and ensuring that they don't get carried away with an inflated sense of their own importance.

Wigeon on Ice

Have simply kept on going
out of all the frosty grass
for no good reason than that

Other wigeon are so doing to
relieve them of the need to
recognise a problem here and so

They push one webfoot out
ahead of them as if it's leaving home
or might be someone else's after all and

Hope the other one will join it in its
own sweet time. An ignominious
glissando. So, as if in slippers,

Never raising heel or toe across the
kitchen floor, they melt it with the
friction of their mass tergiversation,

Scoot, painstakingly, Shove
Ha'penny, together, first
in front and then behind by turns,

Like nudge-nose bows of
Oxford-Cambridge rowing boats at
every pull of oars, un-laughing

At their stand-up, fall-down comedy from
one side to the other – when

Perhaps they might have flown.

The Winter Wigeon

The winter Wigeon
whistle up the marsh,

Whistle up more Wigeon who then
whistle up more marsh to draw it,
apron-strings, around them, with so

Credulous, so ingénue, so artless
and so hardly serious a sound, a pregnable,
incontinent and nugatory note;

Too long at home and full of helplessness – a

Whistle with a squeak that's all-
demanding of attention, nannied, mother-
smothered and un-realised – with

Two holes only
to the hardly tune.
It's wildfowl baby talk.

Though what is this? A
hint of spirit in that second note.
An edge, indeed. Peep petulance.
'It wasn't me, Miss – it was him!'
(And gone the sweetness and the light.)

Whatever next? A simple
variation on a theme?

*

The winter Wigeon
turn and turn about
upon the water. Toy
ducks in the bath, if ever –

Make their own
decision to fly off
at last, leave home, then
losing courage, all fly back.

Goldwater Wigeon

Here is a thing-unearthed out on the marsh;

The sapphire sky set rolling-random as the bottle glass of any Gaudi window in the cool, calypso-beaten antique gold of reed light thick upon the water – with its

Wigeon clasp; white gold and bent, Sun-smith, around his copper head, his pewters and his silvers cooling through him from their black heat while he waits.

Wigeon Sweep the Marsh

Peep-policemen as they go, the Wigeon sweep the marsh,

Investigate it, side to side between the Purslane and the Shrubby Seablite of the wintry

Crime-scene creeks, forensic – holding but a ragged line, as if a

Skein of hobbled geese, eyes down upon a grassy sky and grimly grazing their own

Trail of clues, in unrelenting peep-policemen monotone.

Vintners & Coopers

Godwits go back a long way. Their very name in Anglo-Saxon, *godwiht*, means 'good creature' which implies a certain fitness for the table in times when the value of a wild bird or animal was seen essentially in terms of its ability to stave off hunger.

There are two sorts; Black-tailed Godwits which may be seen in goodly numbers in their winter quarters here, though many spend their whole year with us, and Bar-tailed Godwits which are mostly passage migrants, breeding in the Arctic, but which make themselves apparent from July when they return, right round to May again. The Godstreaming Godwits are the Bar-tailed version which also made it onto the back cover.

Godwits are sizeable waders with an eye-catching length of beak for probing deep in the mud even when they are already up to their rump in pool water, so that it is not uncommon to see a large group with one or the other of them having lost their heads completely at any one time! Black-tails have a beak which keeps to the straight and narrow, whilst Bar-tails have a raised eyebrow of an upward turn to theirs – though both are significantly pink towards the base. The former also sport a white chevron of a wing bar which is strikingly apparent in flight – as the 'Godswarm' photograph shows.

A large flock of godwits passing purposefully close overhead like a fist-in-a-glove is one of the truly woolly-hat wobbling encounters of the saltmarsh. The birds in the aforementioned photo remind me of a swarm of cartoon hornets giving the impression of a single 'sting' between them – never mind that the whole flock would have to turnabout as one in order to deliver it! I can still hear the drawn-out 'hush' of the birds in the panoramic cover image – the hairs on my neck beginning to rise again.

Newly returned from more northerly breeding grounds or even having bred hereabouts, many of these birds have not entirely lost their fructose-rufous breeding plumage. (A significant number may be precocious juvenile birds which nevertheless like to adopt the colouring of the adults in their eagerness to get on with things. It was ever thus.) The Worshipful Company of Vintners, then – a ruby-rich sherry or a coppery cognac perhaps – and Coopers; brandy by the barrel with all of their Autumnal jumping through hoops.

Godstreaming

Birds of a silver scale,
fish of a feather –
birds out of water, for
fish out of air.

Godstreaming; every bird one-or-another with pouring and

The Worshipful Companies

**Pouring at last from the stopcock still spinning when for all of an hour
they have nothing but ruffled their feathers, shuffled their wader-feet –
tide-nudged and wave-nibbled – tipped**

**Off the pebble-spit, rattle-bag,
stones roaring out of a kettle pan,**

**Flipped-over flatfish,
white-bellied, shark-bellied even,
thrown on their back on the watery floor to
a ceiling of nothing but sky and now up again,**

Shoaling, with fins for the rolling,
around again, try again,
settle to being but birds again – all of them

Godwitted, outwitted –

Streaming with consciousness
not of their own to be
flicker-book page-turning,
thumb to the corner and
too quick to read themselves
birds anymore. I am

Whirled on my feet. They are

Rolled up and gone with a flap as they flip
to the rim of a saucer, thin as the squint of an eye in the
glare off the water, materialise like a moth to the light
to be full in my face again, beating my forehead,

Bursting the sky or the sea to its seams.

Godswarm

Sequacious all and dart, spit pips
of itching-powder hawthorn, fired

A-skitter on the hard air – every bird

Nib-tapered to this sky at such and such a point and drawn
to every tingle-smart of water in the nostrils,

Chasing watercolours;

Plum-rusts of a dying day now bleeding backwards through its
aging blotting paper turning at the corners,

Until every bird is finished with a flourish of a
reed-stem pen dragged through a mud-soft tablet –
Babylonian characters. Sumerian. A

Time-charmed swarm upon a
stele of all the sky, although each

Godwit beak attuned and pointer-twanged to
some fey impulse only strong enough to sense between them –
fitful and unsettled, up and down again –

Divining poles or tides or far too many birds upon one scrape:

Whiplash with themselves again,

The whole stung flock.

Good Godwits

Along the saltmarsh finger and its
fainting-mauve-lips, mussel-frill Sea Lavender,

Are acne-pimpled adolescent godwits
all among the adult birds this early back
and following them, one by one,
above my head, to grass-is-greener marshes. Yet

Another peels off from a single oystercatcher's
sticky beak attentions, his up-coming

Cinnamon aglow with copper as the light this
near side of the seawall catches him
until it is no less than his own rusting barrel hoops,
a-clattering behind him that he's flying through.

Godwits in Lavender

A Medieval recipe:

Plum birds, late-summer
dressed, arrived in time
and laid out end to end
along the banquet table

All amongst the lavender.

God whit – good bird,
good thing-to-eat and
netted from the marshes
in their beak-entangled
scores to bend the festive
boards all down the hall.

Like larks in the rafters,
swan, in her very own
feathers again, snipe,
in the grain of the wood.

Godwits in lavender.

Mercers & Haberdashers (pewterers & pattenmakers)

Dunlin are probably the 'default' little shorebird for many of us; the-one-it-is-likely-to-be, the 'little brown job' of the seaside – though there is a great deal more to them that even a slightly lingering eye will detect. We see them mostly in their winter plumage which might legitimately be described as 'dun' (a brownish-grey), but there are always some birds which remain for the summer and can be seen sporting their ink-puddle tummy and chestnutty back.

Dunlin are often seen intermingled with other shorebirds – smaller ones such as Sanderlings as well as Ringed Plovers and Turnstones with which they zip along only just above the surface of the creekwater in a flickering and purposeful flock, or larger birds such as Curlews, Oystercatchers and godwits, whose shadows they seem quite happy to stand about in (for the kudos, no doubt) on a mud or sand bank in the middle of said creek.

I have imagined Dunlin as the mercers (general grocers) or haberdashers (sellers of general sewing bits and pieces) of the coastal fringes bird world, although in the 'Muddypeg Dunlin' poem I have likened them to pewterers and pattenmakers. It also occurred to me that they might make very good actuaries (life assurance calculators) – a 'dun' profession (to all appearances) if ever there was one!

(These almost 'makeweight' birds might easily have found a place in the first book in this series but the very fact that they are so un-fussy about the company they keep means that they have a foot – albeit a small one – in both camps and so justify, I hope, their inclusion in this one.)

Whilst I am very pleased with the visual drama of low light and the tumble of snowy reflections in the main photograph, it is the sub-plot of the single Dunlin left alone on stage which gives this image its peculiarly poignant potency, I think.

Muddypeg Dunlins

Among these once-upon-a-mudbridge stumps;
a Seahenge-woody handful, flung, of
tiny tooth-peg pit props for the sky, twice
inundated by this creekpool water,
second-hand, and gleaming-lit again,

Is all the knock-kneed space in which
a small-time busyness of Dunlin-birds may
bend their spongy-timbered heads, now
lifting lids of shiny tins, now stirring up
with little sticks the gloss blue sky
still runny through their feet; one bird,
a beak that's twice as long. These

Dunlin always gravitate to something
rather than to nothing; every bird
a peg for playing solitaire whilst
taking all their turns at once – so

Bagatelle, as well, they bounce but softly
off and out of one another's space
(however little it may truly be their own).

Worshipful Pewterers; of worthy
mud-slopped tankard grey or
Pattenmakers (every bird the size and
shape of some clog-wooden shoe).

Dunlin Nappin'

Keeps the wide world ticking over
with the one eye open for a moment,
closed – whilst holding me at bay
in our best interests, assigning me a
squint-that-dares-me distance as he
wobbles on a single leg with shuffle-
shifting all his feathers once again –
to drop them into place – so hardly
bothered to be bothered by this
slack-jaw saltmarsh bluster wind.

Fishers & Crabbers

Since those first and occasional and almost incomprehensible sightings 30 or so years ago, the Little Egret has become unashamedly part-and-parcel of the Norfolk wildlife scene.

Along our saltmarsh creeks and in its pools, these distinctly Mediterranean and culturally iconic members of the heron family are now an absurdly common sight – a bird which one is certainly more likely to encounter than not. (For River Nile read 'Morston Quay' and for our own familiar herons with their preference for keeping folks at arm's-length, read now 'Little Egrets' who have happily exploited that once-vacant seal trip channel niche!)

All this increasing familiarity, however, is not to say that the sight of a pristine white egret, home-from-home and flying deep-keeled as a yacht against the setting Sun (they are one of the last birds to call it a day and go to bed) isn't easily enough to oft-times raise a flutter of excitement and the thrill of Ancient Egypt; pyramids, stylised drawings of them on papyrus and the walls of tombs along the Valley of the Kings.

Although it is not too difficult approaching egrets in order to soon find oneself utterly entranced by their snake-neck fishing and crabbing exploits (tiddlers, mostly) all along the creeks, it is another matter photographing them in action so as to not only achieve a sharp image but also to do justice to the softness and differentiation of their monochrome plumage. The light has got to be right. I am pleased with the quite unusual orientation of the Marigold egret which had clearly spotted something as it was passing me by and then suddenly wheeled about to display those astonishingly uncensored feet (allowed only a muddy glimpse-of ordinarily and even then one at a time) in all their saffron glory. I very much like the shadow play upon the fishing egret, the tension in it and the summary reflections.

The Worshipful Companies

Marigold the Egret

Around the last big corner of the

Old tide's air – still stale
with being not flushed through entirely –
shutting sluice gates hard behind her,

Fisher-egret comes on Marigolds to kick-start

Creek-incoming water,

Jiggling up the mud
(where sun doth hardly shine)
on toes like yellow tuber roots – with
lunatic and manic trembling so that

All that is limivorous
(or simply hiding) makes a
potter's-slippy wriggle or a
mud-gloop, would-be scuttle for it to the

Next-door egret's little piece of

Delta Nile – to find asylum
in a Norfolk saltmarsh creek.

Apothecaries, Grinders of Powders & Suppliers to Sawbones

The Shoveler is one of those iconic species which may quite regularly give an extra and unexpected lift to a Norfolk birder's day. It has a real visual and physical presence on the pool. That oh-so-fantastically utilitarian bill might lend an air of ridicule to lesser wildfowl, but its splendidly unfussy colour combination and the fact that it makes absolutely no apologies for its appearance means that the Shoveler is very much its own duck. It seems to span the divide between the more common and plentiful species such as Pochard, Wigeon, Tufted Duck and Teal and those, such as Pintail and Goldeneye, which keep a wary distance.

I had been watching a pair of Shovelers with their young brood on a Salthouse pool when a second male interrupted the idyll by attempting to join in. The familial male dutifully saw him off by swimming after him with the species' curious head-bobbing display and the intruder duly took the hint – for about five minutes. The photo was the unexpected result.

I took multiple shots of the second Shoveler coming in to land right in front of me and was very pleased with this one, not least because of that superlative beak being in good focus - something there is simply no opportunity to see in real time with a bird flying towards you – together, as it happens, with the feet, which helps to give the impression that they are indeed sticking right out so that there is plenty of forward momentum to the picture.

Apothecary

Shoveler incoming –
yellow bead drawn on me,
landing at me any moment now
with every drop of this end of the pool, a
full-tap scoot of water –

Is a tricorn waterfowl; with
ears-and-elbows wings, his own
head hardly doffed upon his body
at such unexpected greeting,
skid-pan feet. Projectile

Duck; blunt-mannered.

Shoveler incoming –
with that shoe-horn,
oboe-reedy flaring,
adze-cum-gouging chisel,
fibreglass extrusion to a
bucket seat of such

A hands-on handful of a beak.

He splashes down his
worshipful apothecary colours
(water briefly rusts and
oxidises – shop bell – with them);
port wine red, white powders
in a folded packet – druggist
poison or placebo – bottles
green upon the shelf. He

Pays us all a visit, gives us all
a taste of his own medicine and
with a snake-upon-a-stick,
a vacuum attachment,

Hose-honk smile.

Teal are pocket-sized ducks which, again, are with us all year round and easily flushed unwittingly from any saltmarsh ditch or pool, any water-meadow puddle-of-a-pond or just as likely come across sitting it out around the edges of a busy scrape – the light drawn to the velvety chestnut and the green-turned-blue, gold-braided, of their heads. Another colourful surprise to their neat plumage is the soft, creamy yellow of their undertail, black bordered and seen properly only when they rise vertically and with great agility in a flurry of water droplets – gone, as if they had a train to catch.

Teal are dabblers like Shovelers rather than up-enders such as the longer-necked Pintail. They are famously paranoid about their nesting arrangements – perhaps unsurprisingly in view of their historic popularity with wildfowlers.

This photo is an excellent example of how an image inspires me to write; the birds entirely grounded and 'at home' in their environment, the resonance of all the colours and the various shines and gleams upon their plumage and the water, the storyline behind the half-glance of the drake back over his shoulder at me.

Bronzewater Teal

The Word is Teal

Upon the bronze face of the Water and its silver – both

But ditch-seam rinsings.

Light comes polishing in circles and the surface of it
gleams with housemaid rub;
The Sun upon his knees.

These ripples are a liquid
consequence of light; now
gorged upon it, they will push and
push their tide-rim margins up against
the limits of this single and
essential waterfowl until
their pattern piles upon him.

Knit with very water-light
(both crochet-hooked and
Fair Isle yarned), the bird is
cast off, tied off, polyp
disengaged to float away
with one last plop, one
duck-cheek finger-pop
and suck – made Very

Flesh and Feather

In the spirit of the thing.

*

Two curling stones, the

Teal turn slowly – pestle
to the mortar – grinding down
their own disturbance to the
surface of the water as they go,

Unhurried and yet gone and gone – the very

Stepping-stones of light.

Drake Pintails are quite the most rakish and elegant of our winter ducks, oozing class, good breeding and impeccable sartorial discernment – not to mention a decidedly mouthwatering, desert-themed colour scheme. The pinched-to-a-point fine-art distinction of their eye-catching winter plumage never seems to go to their head, however. They have no particular airs and graces, and are even a little reserved in their demeanour, limiting any mud-scrape contretemps to those between their own kind and seemingly recognising the wisdom-in-general of toeing the line with the missus on pain of being brought down the proverbial peg or two. I have the sense in fact that there is a slight air of modest wonderment about them, as if they imagine all the fuss must be about somebody else.

This pintail-in-profile, lifting and falling in sympathy with a full and lively swell, with its lacquered beak and every feather settled to its place, epitomises the easy refinement of these waterfowl for me. The prose photo shows just how similarly slimline the Pintail females are, though nesting camouflage is the high priority for them of course.

Ducks' Own Duck

Uncomfortable in his skin to be so effortlessly chic-sartorial designer-labelled. Year after

Year, by popular consent, the ducks' own duck (a waterfowl's own waterfowl, by 'vote of readers of the magazine'), the

Duck to which one may aspire.
Uneasy at the mere suggestion of
his own immaculate conception,

Rests a milk-run 'index finger'
up against his cheek as if in
deep consideration, hurt by the
suggestion when his aspirations
are entirely philanthropic – and, if
anything, are would-be surgical;

His feathers – paper-cuts along his
wavelet-water lifting-and-subsiding back,
a tail to run an opening from head to toe,
already closed – his only instruments,
laid out with light-wink and with polished,
wooden-handle gleam. No sawbones, he.

His is a fine-art surgery; his
gall-stone eye will run a bump
beneath each surface and appearance

And besides, his makeshift, field-theatre is a
muddy scrape he shares with all and sundry –
commoners and clowns – no matter
how he holds his high-born head
through no fault of his own.

Spotted Redshank

So –

What is it? Yes,

I have spotted you, too,
have seen all I need
of you. What can it be that

You are requiring of me which
means that you are still there?

The sense of a bird? Of a life
which is other than yours set loose
inside a sheaf of feathers so
distinguishing of me (apparently) by
pattern or by colour from the next? The
fascination, then, of all my so soon
come-and-gone – on strummed and
clap-percussion wings – as thistledown
upon the wind's licked fingertips to
spin the oceans of the globe to finest rain,
while you must plod upon the earth with
only pencil and with notebook to confine me?

Tick upon your precious list.
(In which case why are you not
also come-and-gone already?)

Voyeur. Gloater at me standing in the
water and the mud up to my knees.

Turn your own head
on its shoulder – see me
only incidentally or
even deferentially

Over it. As I with you.

Cordwainers & Shoehorn Suppliers

If we still regard our Little Egrets as somewhat exotic, how much more so are the Spoonbills? These are much rarer summer visitors (though from only just across the sea – from the wetlands of the Low Countries – and, with the change in climate, on the increase here) with not only the kudos their rarity gives them, but with bags of character as well; that preposterous, shoehorn-like beak, their head-dress plumes, the disconcertingly human gait, their very size – all make for a bird once seen, certainly never forgotten. Storks rather than herons. Chanced upon singly along a tide-drained creek, they are reminiscent of a certain long-legged comedian. Flying in groups of three or four above the saltmarsh, which is more likely, Spoonbills have the airy-winged mystique and jaw-dropping presence of swans.

The thirteen Spoonbills in the panoramic photograph had virtually taken over this mudscape on a saltmarsh pool for the morning. Somewhat affectedly imposing as they went about their preening, heads thrown over shoulders with a snake-like dexterity, it is the understorey of Avocet and Godwit courtiers and retainers and their reflections which makes this image so arresting. That, and the lovely soft light which gives the Spoonbill's plumage such a royal-icing-like consistency.

Beaks Extraordinaire

Thirteen Spoonbills this day at the pool and,
at their masters' feet, two dozen Avocets
with half and half again of only late-apprenticed
summer-sozzled Godwits –

One reflection sleeping-off another:

Fire-tong, steam-press-stamp utensils,
upsy-daisy sewing sailing needles,
finger-licking, dead-eye drills
to pump the mud – all

Smoothing out and skinning,
puncturing the soon-as-maybe,
closing-over, shoehorn shine.

Spoonbill Sneezes (*to a Certain Well-loved National Institution*)

We have stumbled on this retro-entertainment; tripped up
at some mischief with a quick-pulled dinghy rope to find

It is a spoonbill, not an egret,
on the far side of the creek – to find ourselves

Included, ludicrously, in an out-take from
The Ministry of Silly Walks and he
with one eye on me just in case it is the
full-blown twenty-minute argument I'm
wanting (not the five or ten). His beak

Is monstrous kitchenware; a Pythonesque
and joke utensil for the holding of a
baked potato (sea potato, even) at arm's length,
a mudcake spatula or jellyfish transferer.
Or perhaps a keepy-uppy cockle racquet –
ah, a shoehorn (much more likely on reflection)
for a marshman's belt & braces waders
(paddle to be better off without whilst
up the creek this evening). Well, so
much for parrots, once-removed.

He slashes at the water with it as if fed up
with the nettles at the bottom of the garden
(or admonishing the bonnet of a small red car).

He sneezes. (Tiny, lost crustacean
swimming in the nostril-pool.)
His yard of ale of beak springs open as if,
at a snap, unhindered by elastic bands
and all at once I see that they are
nothing but maracas on a stick … so that
it's more to do with playing-on-the-spoons
than sipping at the water from the creek.

His pink eyes pop. His headgear
flares into a bunch of optic fibres and

I am astounded by the recognition that this
spoonbill is more pelican than egret, with his
yellow throat bag flapping to be fed.

He turns his back on our astonishment at
his expense and walks back up the creek bank,
throwing plume-toss glances over shoulders –
left and right – pique-petulant, now

Opens up his wings to fly
and all at once is simply breathtaking by
grand design and straightway
wiping smiles off faces –

Skyful. Not far off a swan.

Quilters & Broderers

Greenshanks are the high-society cousins of Redshanks; elegant, splendidly turned out and with impeccable manners, their good breeding apparent in their very lack of aloofness and disinclination for lauding it over their much commoner creek-mates who would not hesitate, I'm sure, to rub their lengthy noses in it if the (class-pretentious) wading-boot was on the other foot.

Greenshanks breed in the high wilds of the Hebrides and the Scottish Highlands and migrate to the Mediterranean, or even further south for the winter, though a few will stop off on the way and even end up spending longer than they intended to along our coasts – hence this particular bird and two or three others which I was thrilled to come across and then keep track of day by day for several weeks along our Morston creek.

I could count on this bird covering the same length of the main creek at low tide, whenever I was able to visit, meticulously working the water within its compass as it leaned intently out over its surface but then sometimes taking to the air all of a sudden, dramatically swinging out over the water in a complete about turn, calling with an unexpectedly clear and airy piping to land where it had been a half an hour before.

I like this photograph, particularly for the exquisitely quilted texture of the bird's plumage and the apparent 'stitching' together of the feathers of its back so that it might almost be wearing a high-tog Elizabethan doublet – that, and the olive, straight-from-the-jar, green of its legs.

Quixote Bird (*to a Greenshank*)

Bird of the moment – bird
of this winter long.

Between the Moon-poke jetty moorings
and their shanty town of sloping-gangplank
walkway levels (like a fairground fun house
or an Escher optical illusion) treacherous with
mud, still, from the tidal surge, I must appear
and disappear from view as if through
slots around a zoetrope with following a

Single wading bird on long, cod-liver legs
along the draining creek. A pale and
slim-line tonic of an unexpected visitor.

Quixote bird – she simply tips from one leg to the other
as she falls into a run only to stop again at
every small presumption of a fish just missed,

Now tilting at the Redshanks coming up the other way
(though diffident, for they are cousins at the tourney)
or at the reflection of a windmill on the water
(Burnham Overy or Cley) and wearing but a
nearly-smile, her beak up-strung; a
chinstrap for a long discarded helmet,

*

While I lose her in amongst the empty-bottle Brent Geese
rolling from the bank into the water for a better view
until the quick-surrender flash of her arachnid dip
(as easy cantilever keel-and-beak as any
paddle-slapping sprinkler for the field) is
sparked upon their pencil lead. She

Reins herself in hard to dance,
high-stepping, through a
dressage circle on the water,
throws a tiny fish to catch, as
running-light as whetted-arms. There

Is a queue by now for boat trips to the seals.
She flies. She trails her legs of all her
sparkle-pearl, her water-droplet favours,

Turns about to wing her way back up the creek at me, her
tongue-loosed jubilation bouncing off the mud banks as she comes and

Ringing wilder, rounder, fuller of far distant places, clearer
and still surer even than the cries of Redshanks whose
parochial demeanour is betrayed with every note of panic
at each innocent encroachment (xenophobes,
to test the very patience of a long-pulled earlobe).

So she lands and turns to joust at ripples on the
Field of the Cloth of Silver of her own reflection, leans,
to ascertain, myopic, chinks-in-armour in her quarry
just before she lancing-darts and
trips – faux pas, a small inelegance –
upon a mooring rope beneath the water.

*

It is only now, in this grey light,
I understand the essence of her
maiden-muted winter plumage;
warm-air floated, still-soft porcelain
moss-seeded from a Sutherland bog,
pale olivine – a

Quilted doublet stitched from
hardly-tarnished pewter –
faery-fibred tin and lead.

Loriners (manufacturers of bridle, bit and spur)

During the first Spring of my arrival in Norfolk, I was astonished and utterly perplexed by an oddly twanging, all-pervading sound that seemed to fill the wet meadow at the end of the lane which I had taken to exploring. It was a noise that simply could not be ignored – like the coming-and-going plucking of a double-bass string, the source of which I could not, for the life of me, trace. It had a ventriloquist quality to it which had me searching the grasses all around my feet for frogs or similar, frowning hard into watery pools, scanning the fields in the distance for droning and thrumming machinery. When I finally identified it, after several days, as the high-flying, circling, dipping-and-lifting little skylark-like bird way above my head, it was an epiphany moment for a naturalist – and I put my hands to my knees and laughed out loud. It was a Snipe, displaying, the unearthly yet musical sound, out of all proportion to the size of the bird, coming from a pair of sticky-out feathers at the base of its tail vibrating hard in the air as it dived. I have entertained a hearty admiration and affection for these generally secretive, pool-edge-hugging, mud-investigating birds – partway between a wader and a woodcock – ever since.

Loriners, I thought, because of the bridle striping of their heads and all along their backs, although having witnessed snipe zipping up-and-away at a shot-evading (they are still counted as game birds – fair game – sadly) zig-zag lick, there is really not a hope of reining them in!

The main photograph (p.84) is a favourite of mine (I have a large canvas version above my desk) because it reminds me of the water-meadow habitat in which I encountered my first Snipe (though the Water Purslane in the foreground identifies this particular Snipe as a coastal-grazing-marshes bird), but also because it illustrates the Snipe's superb camouflage, the oatmeal stripes along its back almost a continuation of the rootlets behind it. I like the photo of the bird probing the watery mud because of the reflection and because it actually shows the flexibility of the tip of that remarkable appendage of a beak!

With the 'To a Local Snipe' poem (which celebrates that initial encounter), I have used a watermark version of the very first photo I ever took of one, perched on a piece of farm machinery slowly dissolving into the meadow behind the one I've described, early one morning, with a camera I'd only ever taken family photos with before with never a thought of telephoto lenses!

The wet meadow described became a fascination for me, not least because of the amazing variety of flowers such as Water Avens and Marsh Orchids, which could be found there, and before very long, with the help and advice of the Wensum Valley Project as well as the Fakenham Area Conservation Team, it was set up as a local nature reserve known as Gogg's Mill, in deference to its own local history.

To a Local Snipe (*Paean to Gogg's Mill*)

He has left in the middle of packing again, with

Hardly the time for a handful of browns and
a hasty arrangement of streakings of grasses
snatched up at the last: a suitcase, half-closed,
full of pokings and rustlings to potter about in
elsewhere, to try on unseen – the dregs of his
colours still here and still clear in the turn
of the paintwater. Works, Un-Collected,
of a Small Patch of Wet Meadow,
often exhibited. Rarely so seen.

Fled in the last of the night.

All the way up in a panic of flight at an
(out of a milk bottle) fizz-firework gradient,
shaking my stare (which is caught in its flare)
from his shoulders and rolling me loose from his back
('til I'm almost unsaddled). Skedaddled.

Flittering wings in cuttlefish waves
to abandon me, overboard, lose me at sea –

Keelhaul me under the sky,
'til he's won my attention
with every diversion

And sits on his
brownstar meridian.

*

Stalls – and tips, beak wise.

**The sky's full dome gives way
to an involuntary shudder.
Its membrane hums
and trips into a triple beat**

**At which the tree's trunk shivers,
the clouds cringe, and
even the grass lays flat.
A peculiar sound – the Spring's own
flapping, double-bass-string bleat**

**That has us turning heads
in all directions, or towards each other –**

**To our clumsy feet
(where I searched vainly
in the grasses for an hour
when I first came here
all these years ago).**

Stubb Farm Snipe (for The Graingers)

Snipe pudding-plump
the cold-slumped grass

Where ice-blown snow
sits sweating on the
mophead tussocks,
making airy igloos for
old hays and leaves, and

Dwindling to these wet and
crystalising salts-and-
sugars, deliquescent
coconut. The

Snipe are at a loss; the
snow has thrown them off
their own dry scent and
lifted them like children's
transfers floating to the
Earth's slip-surface –

Where they bloat with
February warmth and sit
outside, forgetting how to hide –
their instinct to be shrinking
into those same hays and leaves
and to be wrinkling, vacuum-
packed into their camouflage

Turned inside-out, their
every thought (once
running up and down their
age-long bills, invertebrate
and loose) turned on its

Snow-dumped head.

Snipe (with a water purslane side salad)

All spilled beans and lentils,
pearl-barley, pulses,

Coffee grounds
sloppy with clay slips and creams,

Dribbled and drained between rootlets
and rhubarb-pink water plant stems all but
babbling with succulent tongues –

Seeping their way
into biscuit-crumb soils;
digestives and gingers and
arrowroot plain.

His feathers fall away
like emptied mussel shells
without a clink.

They slip and slither,
tumbling down his back
like shellac counters
– handful after handful –
losing all his outlines for him

While the running edges of them
are the very rootlets, white and blind,
in any open wound of earth.

His eye is a blackberry polyp,
blood-blister blurted
with squeezing his chipmunk-like head
between fingers-and-thumbs of the
space between sedges and mudwater edges
where the gaps are no ginnels,
the ginnels no gaps.

Snipe has swallowed
        a worm-thing
                the length of his beak

(in turn, the length of himself)
as if it's an oyster;
tipping it back, sipping it flat,
slurping it straight from the ground with a flourish to
nourish his camouflage – only the tip of him

Sensitive-pained as a
glistening glans – for the
sightless and light-fingered knowing –

The taste at the drop of a touch.

Barstaff & Bottlewashers

I find Shelduck a bit of an oddball species – as much goose as duck, seemingly comfortable in a wide variety of coastal habitats and yet not quite fitting in properly anywhere. This is probably a little unfair. I do have enough of a fascination with them to have explored their almost 'bottlebank' colour scheme through painting; that dark and brooding seaweedy green which in combination with the scarlet beak, already unwieldy with its knobble in the male, makes the head look so top-heavy and the chestnut band around the linen white which strikes me as somehow reminiscent of a barman or a waiter with a napkin over his forearm.

Perhaps unsurprisingly, in light of the above, Shelduck are often found in the company of geese rather than ducks so that I wasn't exactly surprised myself to find them in such well-organised tandem with the Brent Geese here as I photographed them coming over the shingle bank from the sea – although what did amaze me was the way these unrelated species had co-operated to such a degree as to be responsible for half the V-formation each and so precisely!

If Ever a Goose Was a Duck

Or a duck were a goose – then a

Shelduck is neither the one nor the other,
to every intent and its purpose
is practically both – the

Two for a quick-spinning penny
afloat in their builder's sand buoyancy rings
and the bouncing, white bellies
of gulls out at Sea –
while they dose themselves silly
with viscous and green embrocations
the length of their necks
which will end at a sealing-wax knob

For the pressing of
Push-me and Pull-you
identities:

Goose that is almost a duck which is
not quite, but nearly, a goose.

Two-kinds Skein

A two-kinds skein;
    a blink and double-take of
        brent-and-shelduck wildfowl V –

The sharp-end brent goose only pointing up the way
    for better sharing out the sky, while
        geese and shelduck hold precisely

Half the reins and
    keep their shape – with one, it seems, still
        hardly recognising it is not the other – from

The losing-face
    of breaking loose, the floundering, the
        falling out to all four corners of the sky.

Leapers & Moongazers

Hares are an enigma. They straddle two worlds; the mystical and the all-too-real. So indigenous to these islands as to easily predate our own arrival and so astonishingly well adapted to cope with a life lived entirely out in the open that they retain an aura of magic and mystery, commanding, historically, our deep respect as the ultimate survivor – a special relationship enshrined in Celtic and Medieval myth. Perhaps the true wonder of hares, however, is that they have managed to continue to thrive into the present day, despite our depredations of the natural world and despite our pursuing them to exhaustion in our very fascination with them in the name of sport – not so much by crossing over into our own world but by existing parallel to it, alongside it, taking advantage of the kind of habitat afforded by traditional farming practices and even managing to adapt to our far more intensive agricultural policies – nowhere more apparent than in Norfolk. It is almost as if hares have more of a stake here than we do. What an heretical and schismatic thought!

Even so, it may well be that our more enlightened thinking on the matter – with the provision of set-aside around our fields and the re-instatement of hedgerows not so very long ago grubbed-up – has come only just in time.

Brown hares (there are also Mountain, or Blue, hares – a different species), originally a down-land animal but familiar, as we've noted, to field and pasture, have also become quite at-home on our coastal grazing meadows in the lee of the shingle bank and even in the sand dunes, way out at Blakeney Point itself. It is not inconceivable that in future millennia there may have evolved a sub-species of Dune or Sand Hare with paws particularly well-suited to the shifting sand underfoot!

The close-up studies of hares were taken on Havergate Island in Suffolk (though only just down the road and which I hope I may be forgiven for) where, due to its very isolation, the hare population has traditionally had little to fear from Man. As a result, the animals are extraordinarily approachable. The other photographs were taken on my own Cley & Salthouse patch.

Albrecht, the Hare

Drawn to a hare – like Albrecht.

This one looking to be such an icon, such
an after-image, station of the artist's cross in
all the years to come but with a photograph –

Still waiting to be told that he may
jump down from the table, so to speak.

At one time any artist who was worth his salt had
Holy Roman emperors and not-so-holy popes to
sweeten with a new pieta or madonna or nativity or
other Bible story fantasy – or, just as inappropriately,
nudes from Greek mythology. Young

Albrecht, though, found
time to draw a hare – and hands
(not only praying ones) and feet,
And, yes, the odd self-portrait in
a bizarrely Newcastle United hat –
although his coup de grâce was not the
Son of God, or Eve or Adam even, but –

Still dripping soil with being
pulled out of the very earth –

A piece of turf.

(Which takes some beating, even
now, as installation, let alone
an altar piece – God's handiwork
as much as any pickled cow.)

Hare Quins

So fit-and-start and circle-crop the
grazing-meadow grass, that it is

Flattened with them all, is
spun – their fun not written on their
faces (lagomorph inscrutable)

But by their ears; their
lopping, Morris-minor indicator,
clashing softly, black-spot ears.

(The ditch which separates us may as well be
post-and-rail for me to lean upon – they have my
distance easily.) And so I watch and

Scrutinise to ascertain the rules of play for
such a game of rounders needless of a bat and ball, to tell, to
separate the players, hare from brown-fur hare: this

Spring quartet, in rough-and-tumble ring
of jumpy starts and nervy fits and

twitchy turnabouts-on-sixpences, of pogo-stick,
of spit-and-sparring cat-and-mouse – 'til
one hare spins apart to play conductor and begins

Careering through a set of ever-tightening loops-for-hoops, is

Leaning hard against the basket-weaving grass to
rope in all the boys and girls (a racing yacht
around a buoy), her paws as ready-toed
as chestnuts fallen open, hind legs
scarifying mud from meadow, ears
a garbled semaphore. And

Suddenly she's done.
She touches base, it seems.
For no apparent score.

So – everybody sits
with amber eyes aglow
and waits for more.

The Worshipful Companies

Hare Tryst

Two hares
in the hardly-light

Fair met in secret but
giveaway – pinned to the
long-running brow of the field
that was oft-times a hill, by the
drain of the dark to the sea.

I am sunken below them,
deep in a bend of the road –
watching them, nervous,
Spring-loaded and
first-time Mad March.

They are going through the motions
(up and down from classroom chairs
around the high school dance floor walls)

Facing one another,
turning, both, away, then
running, one around the
other, giving chase and
keeping distance – saving face
and losing it again at once
with having no idea of
what to say. He, off-hand,

On. She gently cuffs him
for his gross temerity –
can't believe she has and
neither, barely injured, oh, but
wounded to the core,

Can he.

Shelduck & Hare *from 'The Blakeney Point'*

A small truth percolates that I have
learned a thing about the dawn; it's not
so much the stain of light upon the sky
(as if drawn from the Sea by chromatography)
as how the stars begin to dim all by
themselves while it is still quite dark. I

Walk out barefoot to the edge of water
easily a hundred yards away again. The
Sea came in, then, while I slept,
and drew away once more. I don't
remember being conscious of the sound of it
so nearly all-enveloping me, a merely
dune-swell roll of sand away. A

Scivvying of Little Terns stands over
thin and choppy water where two
currents must be meeting – one
unhappy to be slipping underneath the
other, clapping fish into the air so that the
terns are in a quandary; they only know to dive –
and here is breakfast on a plate!

An inch and maybe five miles in from
the horizon is a string of Scoters; an
interminable line of little black-bead,
sea-pup ducks that keep so low they
seem to be unthreading through the
swell-and-trough of waves as birds are
briefly lost to suddenly appear again.

Another abacus-worth of them – so
rattling through my line of sight, so
sagging momentarily and then pulled
tight (to surely cause a pleasant
thrumming down the line), it's
pointless to be counting them. The
scoter train reminds me of my father.

'How long is a piece of string?' he
often used to say. I stride back

All across the smooth, wet sand which
sea-potato froths with soggy clouds of spume
quick-sliding on their cushion of thin water
past me. I break camp to find my hare.

The Worshipful Companies

I sit atop the highest dune; a
carpet-baggy sand volcano,
marram-choked and spiky,
spilling over my bare feet with
all my climbing up it – one
step in and prickled
on the tender sole and
carried down two floors
with simply standing still.

From here I may spot hares.
I have not seen a single one
across this samphire-toggled,
saltlick, mud-crust pan that has
the perfect right by now
to call itself 'dry land'. A

Shelduck party that's been
trying to regroup since I stepped
out into the open – bathroom-china white
and bottle-banking time and time again
along the dune crests
of this sandy-castle ring –
have found their gum-pink feet at last;
their colours, heavyweight as towels
dragged, sopping, from the sloppy sand,
the male birds' knob of beak, a
sealing-wax accessory. There

Is a hare! A large one, ginger-biscuit brown
and loping somewhere I can tell that I will
struggle to remember for the sameness
of these pock-blown dunes – and giving no
suggestion of expended energy. I
scramble down and fill my boots with
more companionably chasing sand.
I bet he knows exactly where I am.
And so that I am in no doubt,

He swings a single ear upon a
ball-and-socket at me –
Stops me in my tracks.

What now?

Dune Bathers & Floaters 'The company of sun and hot sand worshippers'

Between popular Holkham and my own favourite spot, Burnham Overy Staithe, there is a notable and quite remarkable hinterland of coastal dunes which may be easily explored – a wilderness habitat all of its own to wander for an hour or two. During mid-to-late summer one is more likely than not to bump into Dark Green Fritillaries here – big, hot-orange butterflies flying purposefully one way and then, having maybe forgotten something, the other, strident on the eye – especially on the landward, sheltered side of the dunes.

It is the underside which most readily separates the three largest fritillaries we have in our islands – the Dark Green, Silver-washed and High Brown – although the last is very rare and not found in Norfolk anymore, the former can soon be told apart with practice.

In this photo that green flush (not particularly 'dark', I admit) can just be appreciated beneath the silvery-white spots and dabs on the undercarriage of the butterfly as it probes for sweetness in amongst the anemone-like thistle inflorescence only slightly thicker than its own watch-spring tongue. The spots-before-the-eyes are an intriguing feature of some butterflies.

The feisty and absolutely no-messing-about Wall butterfly is another dune bather – as is the Grayling which almost immediately reverts to the horizontal in order to assimilate itself into its sandy background colours so that the underwing is all one ever gets to see, if one is lucky. The underside of the Wall, by contrast, is hardly ever apparent for long, so easily disturbed is the butterfly at even the most subtle of approaches, although the reward for perseverance and good luck is a glimpse of some unexpectedly fine and colour-washed patternings.

Elbows in the sand to get such detail for the Grayling, but obeisance only on my knees for the Wall butterfly photo.

The Holkham Dunes Fritillaries (*Diary, July 28th*)

I know already of a
cul-de-sac of buckthorn
where the thistles are by
crook-of-arm protected from
the sea winds through the infant,
spade-and-bucket dunes across a
well-trod path which keeps the
roaring Holkham pines in step.

And here there are fritillaries;
Dark Green ones, every year,
resplendent tawny orange,
inky-stylus scratched in black
and potters'-slipped in green with
silver drops of glaze-still-wet
upon their slow-clap underwings

All caught-up in a whorl of
Summer thistle-warmth and
one another; Peacocks, Admirals
and Painted Ladies – Blues, in
all the yellow-riddled sward.

This year, in late July, I'm
starting out from Burnham Overy to
see if I can find them in the marram dunes –
the head-toss, spoke-flail grasses sewn in
mare's tail bunches through the
would-be shifting sand – and

Here is one; a picnic-thoughtless toss of zesty orange peel, un-zipping and now zipping-up the giant-caterpillar tufts on each side of a sand-slip path from top to bottom of the dune. She settles once, she settles twice upon a full-tossed marram braid and clips it, tangerine adornment, four wire insect legs full-sprung bestraddling half a dozen errant twangs of marram – finger in the desert dyke. I

Pin her down to where she glows as if a gem of polished agate slipped from that same finger, lost, suspended in a wickerwork of air, while my own calves are scratched from heel to hamstring with a fricassee of fine white lines. It is apparent

As I wind around and roller-coaster up and down, drop into thump-blast cavities and wind-spun cleaves ingratiated with a choke of bramble, hart's-tongue, pea and willowherb, that

Many of them have seen better days; their orange faded with their black into a bleached and tie-dyed intimation of a former glory. Even at the thistle sanctuary, it's the same – so few fritillaries aflame. Most water-doused, themselves, upon these smoking flower heads. Our summer early. One fritillary has

Taken my attention, though: still
bright and beeline, back towards
the treeline – where the pioneering
maritimes come stepping, tentative,
into the sand and she, now flickering,
intriguing low between the drop-cones
and the litter-twigs, the kneeling-moss,
the bright pink centaury and crunchy
balls of tumble-weeding lichen,

Takes herself on Walkabout
amongst the ankle-scratch detritus
so that she is doused beneath the
tinder where I lose her, re-ignited when
she reappears, a porter on an expedition
carrying her own frail finery (upon
her head) while through my camera lens
I enter her Lost World dimensions –
now a petal stegosaur and now
a Spanish galleon in full sail and
rocking. She has found her island;

One small – barely palm-sized –
purse of violet leaves, quite
summer-shrunken, quilted-close against
the ground, their inflorescence long since gone

Upon which, as I watch, she lays her eggs.

I pick myself up, sated, hardly able
to believe what I have seen, the
giant dunes an almost-insignificance.
I need the whole big Sistine sky above
the sea, the long and dog-leg bank to
jink me, one way and the other,
to the car – to bring me back.

Painted Ladies are aristocrats – that is, they are members of the family of larger and more immediately impressive butterflies which includes the familiar Peacock and Red Admiral. Like the Red Admiral, Painted Ladies are in fact migrants. Nearly all of the butterflies we see on our garden buddleias have made the annual pilgrimage from the Continent and North Africa on deceptively durable and powerful wings but will not survive the winter here. (Some will be second generation insects from early arrivals that have successfully bred during the Spring.) Perhaps because of the long migration they undertake together, Painted Ladies have a strong 'flocking' instinct. I have seen up to thirty of them spinning and chasing and cavorting together in high summer.

I like this photo for the dramatic contrast between the apparent flimsiness of the butterfly's wing and the unforgiving architecture of the Sea Holly. It shows the subtly beautiful patterning of the underside as well – literally, the other side of the coin to the hard-hitting orange, black and white of the topside view.

The Worshipful Companies

Sea Holly

Low in the sharps-
box marram grass
(pins-beneath-the-
fingernail) another
Tudor rose of thorns,
grows blood-let pale
as penicillin mould,

Right royally and
plush-pomade with
fragrant lavender –
enough to crowd a
tiny populace into
its single nosegay – and

Yet every herbs-for-
dinner bishop's crown
arriving at-a-point at
every opportunity with
whirling ball-and-
spike mentality; these

Caltrop, pike
machicolations for
the foot unwary,
for the picnic-happy
palm – enough to keep
the very Sea at bay.

This Painted Lady
makes a pretty point;
with all her flushed and
Spanish Moon-map graces
ratified upon a foreign shore.

Our prickly sand dunes
are an ever-open door.

Grayling

Bares her soul
with no more than
a blink – of startled
eye through shutters,

Flips, old jukebox 45,
to lose her shadow,
giveaway, beneath her
pillow in the sand.
No sundial she, to
be untimely taken –
only flies at-all because she
seems to have the means.

Yashmak – her own veil
pulled to a peep, a
cinders-shaken scarf
wrapped to a smudge
against the heath-ash
sand as grey as that
beneath the pier (dirt
cold) though this
sand hot between the
marram dunes. The

Yin and yang
of hindwing like
the handle of the
brush to fit the
sand-scoop pan,

Her bare-faced cheek
upon bare ground to
shapeshift even, shrink
into herself and slip
between the very grains
if it were possible
and scale by scale.

The Worshipful Companies

Off the Wall Butterfly

First-glance 'fritillary' whose eye-poke at you at the very thought, tells quite a different tale;

No-nonsense, ground-strokes butterfly in orange; turning sun-splashed shadow-spokes upon a lit-stone face or hot-piled dune or high-rise, strut-umbellifer (or any similar excuses for a wall). No

Poser, though, no stretch-recumbent in the sandy set-aside, no sufferer of fools with their own shadows, off the lead – but 'been there,

Done that, let's get all this sunshine business sorted, shall we?'

Off the very wall.

Furriers & Small Mammal Re-packagers

From time to time along our coast and at the seasons' turn, we have large winter influxes of Short-eared Owls. These are irruptions or overflows from the Continent rather than annual migrations and are linked primarily to the fluctuations in the population of voles which are their staple prey. Ephemeral they seem and other-worldly, almost, as a giant moth and all at once apparent, floating just above the coastal marshes –wings up high above their heads in silent concert – when a moment ago there was nothing but a flurry of Redshanks or a circling Curlew-on-a-string.

The 'ears' are merely feather tufts. It is the amber eyes alight in a moon-mask face as the owl's head turns to take you in upon its passing which remain as such a strong impression; the simple sense of momentary contact, fleeting in the extreme for the bird, but which these wild encounters are, nevertheless, all about for me.

The main image here conveys, I think, a sense of the utter intensity of the bird's purpose – brushing my presence aside almost in pursuit of higher priorities at this brief and unlikely point in time.

The photograph of the owl against the Sun setting behind the seawall out from Blakeney I like very much for what the last light has elected to pick out, to draw attention to, within the late October evening air, as much as the definition and the detail of the owl itself which it has not.

My Hand to Stop the Sun (Diary, October 31st)

My hand to stop the Sun
against my seeing him and
every spun thread strung
like time-lapse starlight, hung

In fineline hammock-swags,
upsweeping him from one
end to the other of this
ankle-turning, sickle-graze,
this wilderness gone running
in between the seawall and
the shingle bank – against
some owl-unseemly fall.

Last, late October air
exposed for what it is;
a-choke with all the
hot-breath summer's
dust and debris – husk
and speckle seeded,
mote magnificent with

All the year not quite
gone down – but every
Short-eared Owl now
hounding daylight for
its blessing on each
sun-scratched recitation of

The well-versed drop –
at no more than a sound.

Short-eared Owl

Across the marsh, the

Long, slow handclap of a bird more like

A mist-conjectured,
dusk-light-conjured moth.

Here is a worthy exercise
in flying head to toe;

Tap the head with both hands,
touch the toes – no bending, now.

An opportunist owl.
Camp-follower of voles;
(tomorrow, here or
hereabouts if not today).

Meanwhile, these ears –
one more bad-feather day, though

Eyes still blazing bronze;
stir-crazy dregs, defiant,
indefatigable in between
black-armband wrists –
his checkpoint signal to
slow down and halt.

We cross the Moon with heavy metal here
(palms with silver, summer long) with
transport planes which, sagging-bellied,
slow-and-somehow, keep afloat. This

Owl has trouble staying down, much like a
lead boot diver who would bob away
into a tiny point to break the surface of the
water – or the very circle of the sky.

*

Once, upon a Northern Isle and where there
are but post-and-wire-strung fences
and the whitewashed cottage gardens
are the treeless moor itself,

A Short-eared Owl stood hovering
upon a studied tussock vole,
long seconds while I
readied myself through the
wind-down window that would
hardly do so, of the startled car,

Until a kitten-cat leaped out
from in between the patio pots
to play at Short-eared Owls, or
voles – and spoil that once-in-a
my-own-lifetime photograph.

Lamp Owl

Black gannets on a milk sea
and a pebble's up-and-over throw
across the shingle bank, the
Short-eared Owl comes
running on the seawall rail.

Against the ceaseless flow
of silhouetted, runic figures
(in their twos and half-a-dozens
with their bicycles and dogs)
and all the long way back again,
he sweeps the stale air out
from underneath the
edges of the saltmarsh,

Catches up the corners
of his square cast net and
draws them all together,
concentrating voles. He

Twists – a squirm of spin –
to shutter up the sky from
top to bottom and with
sudden barn-door wings
collapses like a gate-leg table.

*

Barrel-organ owl comes
rolling, winding up to
every turn and turn again,
in its turn – making not so
merry music in the grasses,

Making short shrift
of the lives of voles.

(His face itself a tin-can lid
hung open on his neck, a
lamp-eel's sudden latch
upon the very thought of it.)

*

Two owls now –
crosshatching
this rough grazing,

Dark, dream-tinder owls
against the Empire of the
Sun now setting hugely in
fizz-raspberry and orange-pink,
afloat with people unaware of
being on another planet for a
moment – or of owls.

Bleachers & Dyers

Throughout the Summer, fingertips stretched back to Spring and well forward into Autumn, Blakeney Quay is characterised by crabbers at their craft. It is a family fix – a Norfolk seaside holiday quite inconceivable without the quayside crabbing session. Seal trips and dinghies in the harbour, sand and sea can wait. Sprint down, grab a good spot by a mooring straightaway and only half unpacked and that's the first and most important box of one's essential holidaying happily ticked off. Everyone can now breathe easy. It's a fascinating and disarming thing; grown-up youngsters fresh returned from university and dropping every affectation to be sitting next to small, annoying siblings with a crab line in their hands.

There are gulls about, of course, getting in on the act and in the way – filling the gaps in the picture, the soundtrack; Black-headed Gulls and Herring Gulls mostly and so taken-for-granted in such a holiday playtime context that they are hardly worthy of any attention in their own right, so that any slightly more unusual individuals within the general melee are often passed over completely. Lesser Black-backed Gulls – cousins of Herring Gulls, rather smaller versions of the chick-gobbling, skua-chasing Greater Black-backed Gulls. It is the colour of their legs which sets them immediately apart for me – rings bells in my eyes at once. A surprisingly creamy banana yellow – and in complete contrast to the pink of the Herring Gulls, the red of the Black-headed Gull. They are impressive birds and as there are only ever two or three at a time it is always worth keeping track of them for a few minutes – weaving in and out of the other gulls, the moored-up boats and the milling crabbers – in order to get a sense of their style, their mastery of the air and the water in a confined space, their definite superiority in the pecking order.

Bleachers & Dyers for the stainless, laundered white of their pillow-plump bodies, their emulsion-dipped legs.

These are such smart and dignified-looking gulls. The pose of this one on the rooty, dribbling mud at the creek bank lip and the contrasts between the pristine white, that extraordinarily lickable yellow and the dark slate back make for a very satisfying image, I think.

Yellowlegs Gulls (Lesser Black-backed Gulls)

Not a whelk's throw
from the quayside crabbers
(on their knees or letting out a line
between their heel-clonk wellies)

There are gulls less-ordinary
with their yellow legs upon the
water, reeling in their own
reflections which are those of
neither Herring or of Black-head Gulls –
but Lesser Black-backed Gulls and
all un-noticed with the expectation of
such close-at-hand and loud-mouthed
opportunists being only seagulls,
necessarily. Swung-on-a-

String's-end, low to glimpse the
crabs a-struggle from the bucket
or stood yellow-legged and pegged
upon the opposite bank. Pirates;
freebooters the lot and mercenary,
cheek-by-jowl with Treasure Island,
Norfolk Coast adventurers, un-realising.

Ice cream legs of soft banana.
Brown-skinned knees
a-knobble on the quay.

There is actually a species known as the Yellow-legged Gull but which is associated only with the Mediterranean, so not to be confused!

In Worshipful Company

All rise – in their own time – and
once and once and once again, the

Hushing-sky and staining chromatography of species

Each with its one narrow band of
all the rainbow's spectrum in its gift

Now separating out and out and out into the air.

Other Nature Books by Brambleby Books

Norfolk Wildlife – A Calendar and Site Guide
Adrian M. Riley
9781908241047

Butterfly Gardening
Jenny Steel
9781908241436

Making Wildlife Ponds
Jenny Steel
9781908241481

The Greater World of Little Things
Ross Gardner
9781908241382

Scilly Birding – Joining the Madding Crowd
Simon Davey
9781908241177

The World of Birds and Laughter
Richard Pople
9781908241375

Rings in the Shingle – Images and Poems from the Norfolk Coast
Stuart Medland
9781908241160

Flying High – Discover the poetry in British birds
Anneliese Emmans Dean
9781908241504

Those with Webbed Feet – All about the British Ducks, Geese and Swans
Edward Giles
9781908241573

Walking with Birds
Colin Whittle
9781908241351

Bonkers Birding
John Lee
9781908241542

Sheer Cliffs and Shearwaters – A Skomer Island Journal
Richard Kipling
9781908241214

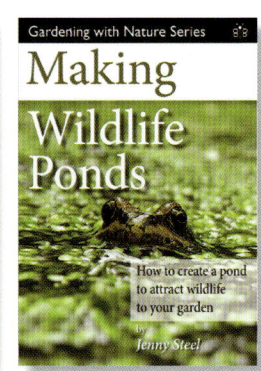

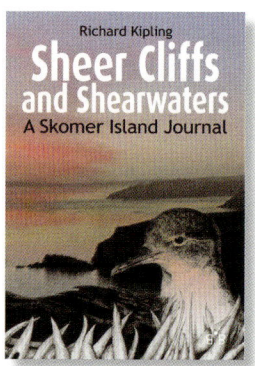